AF606932

Life in the Original 13 Colonies

Audrey Ades

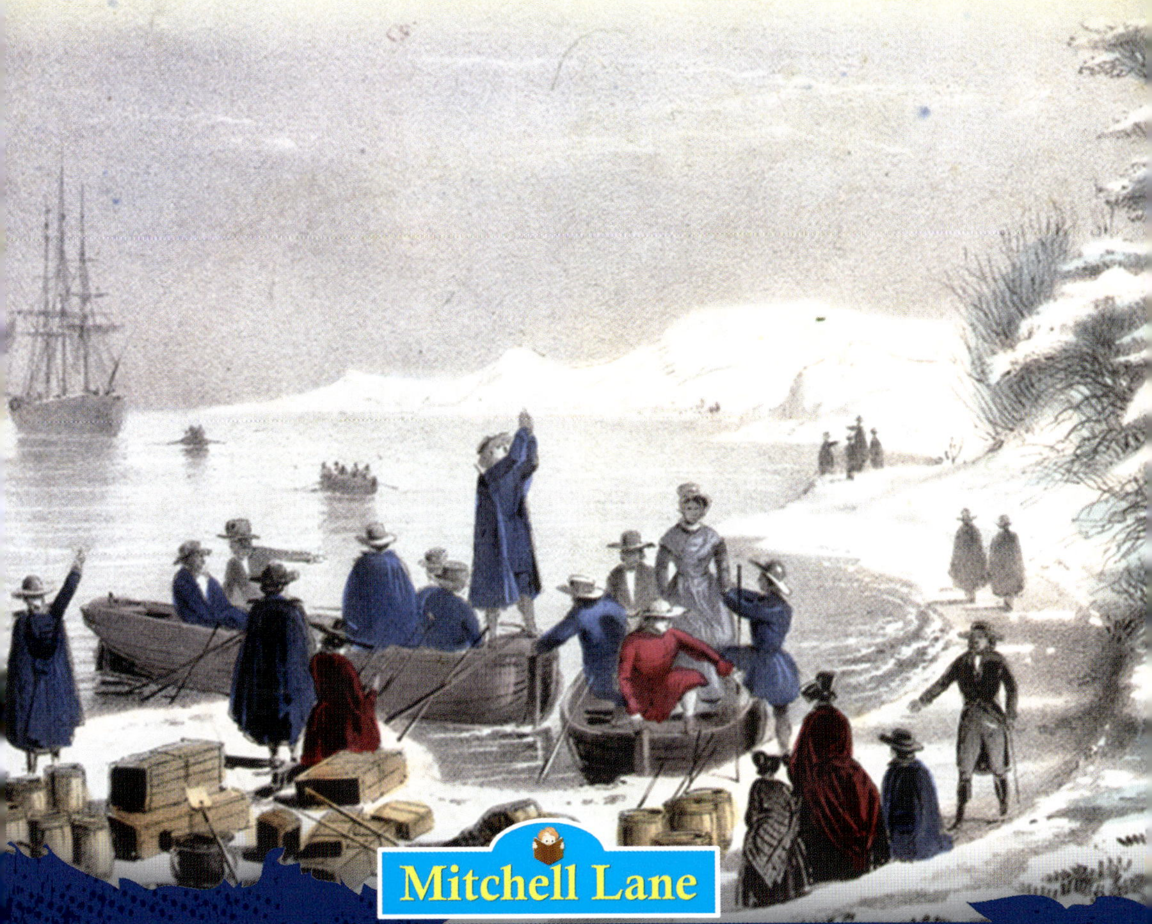

Mitchell Lane
PUBLISHERS
2001 SW 31st Avenue
Hallandale, FL 33009
www.mitchelllane.com

Printing 1 2 3 4 5 6 7 8

The First Continental Congress
The French and Indian War
Life in the Original 13 Colonies
The Second Continental Congress
Stamp Act Congress
The Story of the Declaration of Independence
An Overview of the American Revolution
Who Were the Signers of the Declaration of Independence?

Library of Congress Cataloging-in-Publication Data
Names: Ades, Audrey, author.
Title: Life in the original 13 colonies / by Audrey Ades.
Other titles: Life in the original thirteen colonies
Description: Hallandale, Florida : Mitchell Lane Publishers, 2018. | Series: Young America | Includes bibliographical references and index.
Identifiers: LCCN 2015003201 | ISBN 9781612289892 (library bound)
Subjects: LCSH: United States—History—Colonial period, ca. 1600–1775—Juvenile literature.
Classification: LCC E188 .A27 2017 | DDC 973.2—dc23
LC record available at https://lccn.loc.gov/2015003201

eBook ISBN: 978-1-61228-990-8

CONTENTS

Words in **bold** throughout can be found in the Glossary.

The *Mayflower* arrived in the dead of winter. In this picture, a Native American watches as the Pilgrims come ashore and gather wood. The Indians had bad experiences with white explorers in the past but they were willing to give these newcomers a chance.

1

A New Beginning

Imagine traveling across a wind-tossed ocean to begin a new life in an unfamiliar land. Do you think you could leave nearly everything and everyone you know behind in exchange for such an adventure? Starting in the early 1600s, this is precisely what many English people did. Soon they were joined by people from other European countries.

Sea voyages in the 17th century were difficult and dangerous. They took eight to 12 weeks. Passengers spent this time sharing close quarters with pigs, horses, their belongings, and other cargo bound for the New World. Many never reached their **destination**. Diseases like **smallpox** and **influenza** claimed many lives. Seasickness and poor food left the others weak and unhealthy.

Those who took such a risky voyage did so in search of something they could not find back home. Some sought steady work to support their families. Some looked for gold or other riches. A few were paid to explore the new land and claim it for their kings. Many came in search of religious freedom. Gradually, between 1607 and 1732, most of the land along the eastern seaboard was divided into 13 colonies.

CHAPTER 1

Jamestown

In 1607, a group of Englishmen—no women—founded the Jamestown colony in what we now call Virginia. Their voyage was paid for by the Virginia Company, a group of wealthy **investors** who thought the New World might have undiscovered gold. The settlers were promised a share of the profits in return for their work.

But with profit as their motivation, the settlers spent more time digging for treasure than planting crops for food and building sturdy shelters. Many were from wealthy families and weren't used to the hard work required to survive in an unsettled land. The Native Americans living in the area tried to help them. But instead of accepting their help, the newcomers threatened and attacked them.

As a result, the Jamestown settlers had very little food. **Invoking** the motto, "Work or Starve," Captain John Smith, their leader, insisted that the men spend at least four hours each day farming. One story says that two settlers were tied to posts and left to die as punishment for raiding their meager stores of foodstores.[1]

Smith restored peace with the local Native Americans, many of whom belonged to the Powhatan tribe. A young Powhatan woman, Pocahontas, is credited with saving Smith's life when he was captured and threatened with execution.

Despite Smith's leadership, all but 38 of his men died by the end of the first year. For a short time, the settlers respected the native people. In return, the natives helped the settlers plant corn and other crops. In the following years, more settlers arrived at Jamestown, including some women. The colony grew slowly even though hunger and disease continued to take their toll.

The settlers never found enough gold to satisfy their investors. In 1624, King James I took over the colony. Virginia became the first royal colony in the New World.

Plymouth

Unlike the Jamestown settlers, the 102 passengers who sailed aboard the *Mayflower* in 1620 were not in search of gold. Forty were Puritans, who did not follow the teachings of the Church of England. They wanted desperately to live in a land where they could worship freely. They hoped to establish a settlement which was a "beacon of religious light, a model of spiritual promise, a citty upon a hill."[2] The other passengers belonged to other faiths or left England for reasons other than religious freedom.

The Pilgrims, the term for all the passengers on the *Mayflower*, had permission from King James I to set up a colony near Jamestown. But the ship got lost. In November, 1620, it landed at Cape Cod, Massachusetts.

Before getting off the *Mayflower*, the Pilgrims signed an agreement declaring that they would govern themselves based on the opinions of the majority of the men in the settlement and for the common good of everyone in the colony. This agreement is called the Mayflower Compact.

The voyagers found an abandoned village left by a Wampanoag tribe who had **succumbed** to disease carried by earlier European explorers. This spot had cleared fields and a fresh water source, making the job of starting a settlement much easier for the Pilgrims than if they had to clear the land themselves. They called it Plymouth, after the English port from which they had set sail.

Despite their best efforts, an extremely harsh winter claimed the lives of all but 44 of the original Pilgrims.

Those who survived owed their lives to the kindness of the local Native Americans who provided them with food and shelter during the most **dire** times. Especially helpful was Squanto, who taught the Pilgrims how to fertilize the stubborn northern soil with dried fish remains and grow native corn.

Despite the terrible loss of life, not a single survivor returned to England when the *Mayflower* headed back the following spring. They were here to stay.

Maryland

By 1625, Charles I was the king of England. George Calvert, also known as Lord Baltimore, was well liked by the new British ruler. But Calvert was Catholic and did not follow the teachings of the Church of England. Because he was a friend of the **monarch**, Calvert and his family were allowed to practice their religion. But he wanted all Catholics to be able to worship freely. He set his sights on the New World.

Early in 1632, King Charles granted his friend 12 million acres of land around Chesapeake Bay. Calvert named it Maryland, in honor of Charles's wife Queen Henrietta Maria. When Calvert died unexpectedly a few weeks later, his son Cecelius took over the grant. To attract Catholics, Cecelius sold them large **tracts** of land at very little cost. Many settlers signed on with hopes of making money from the region's long growing season and rich soil.

Cecelius promised religious tolerance for all Christians, including Quakers and Puritans. He made it illegal for members of any religion to **convert** members of another religion. He also declared that no one could argue about religion in public.[3]

The Maryland settlers brought horses, hogs, and honeybees to start their new economy. They also accidentally brought rats that stowed away on their ships. European rats were bigger and more aggressive than native rats. Once they escaped from the ships, they destroyed the settlers' first crops, along with the food that the Native Americans had stored for the winter.[4]

The colonists sailed across the Atlantic Ocean with pigs, cows, sheep, and goats to provide them with milk and meat in the New World. They didn't realize that large European rats had also come along for the ride. These uninvited passengers ate the crops the colonists and the native people counted on to feed themselves.

The settlers also brought smallpox, the flu, and chicken pox. These diseases claimed many lives, especially among Native Americans, who had never been exposed to these germs. Malaria, a disease spread by mosquitoes, also contributed to the deaths of one in five Maryland settlers. Twenty years after the first settlement, there were still fewer than 400 Englishmen in the colony.

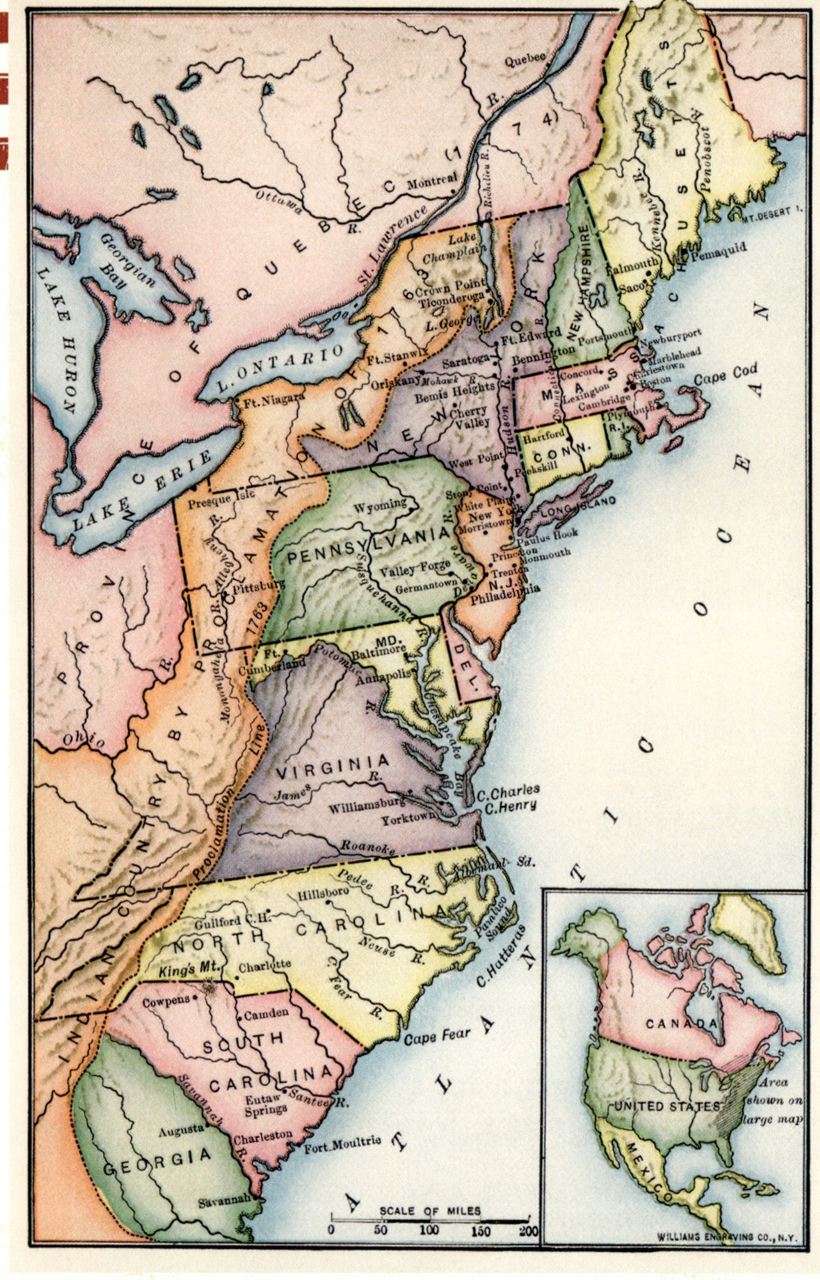

The original 13 colonies spanned the eastern seacoast from Maine (which was part of Massachusetts until 1820) to Georgia. Colony boundaries were often vague, sometimes causing tension and conflict among the settlers.

2 Everyday Life

The years immediately following their arrival were the most difficult for the settlers. But as time went on and more settlers arrived, daily life got easier. They built permanent homes, churches, and schools. Farms for growing crops dotted the landscape. Animals provided meat, dairy products, and hides. Many of colonists ran successful businesses and made clothing and furniture.

But even the simplest chores took a long time. There was no running water, no toilets or showers, no electricity. There was also no such thing as "fast food!" If a family wanted meat, they had to hunt and shoot an animal, skin it, clean it, and cook it over an open fire. The colonists either had to make many items in daily use themselves or trade with neighbors for them. Cloth had to be spun from wool shorn from sheep. They made soap from animal fat. Although some supplies came from England, especially in the early years, these supplies were expensive.

By 1732, there were 13 American colonies, all under the control of the English crown. They were divided into three geographical areas: New England Colonies, Middle Colonies, and Southern Colonies. Settlers often moved to colonies that were the most sympathetic to, and understanding, of, the reasons they left Europe in the first place. Because of these differences, each group of colonies, and sometimes even individual colonies within a group, had different values, beliefs, and practices.

New England Colonies: Massachusetts Bay (including Maine), Connecticut, New Hampshire, Rhode Island

Most New England settlers came in search of religious freedom. Particularly in the early years, each settler had to belong to a family. No one was allowed to live alone. Single or widowed women were expected to marry and have children. Many families had five or more children. Benjamin Franklin, born in Massachusetts in 1706, had 16 brothers and sisters![1]

Women worked in and around the home. In addition to preparing and cooking food, they made the family's clothing and cleaned the house. It was not unusual for women to care for several children under the age of 6 as they went about their work.

The duties of men and older boys varied according to where they lived. Those who had settled along the shores fished, built boats, or made netting and other necessary items for fishing or whaling. Puritan minister Francis Higginson, who arrived in Massachusetts in 1629, noted the abundance of fish:

> There is a Fish called a Basse [bass], a most sweet & wholesome Fish as ever I did eate, it is altogether as good as our fresh Sammon [salmon] . . . Of this Fish our Fishers take many hundreds together, which I have seene lying on the shore to my admiration; yea their Nets ordinarily take more then they are able to hale [pull] to Land, and for want of

Boats and Men they are constrained [forced] to let a many goe after they have taken them, and yet sometimes they fill two Boates at a time with them.[2]

Fish was an important part of the colonists' diet. With no refrigeration, fish that were not eaten right away were dried and salted to keep them from rotting. Dry salted fish could last 6 months or longer.

Those who lived inland raised the town centers and worked in shops. Almost all had a farm to grow their food and, if they were lucky, produce a little extra to sell.

Disease, infection, and the harsh conditions of colonial life took the lives of many babies and young children. Surviving children were expected to work to help the family as soon as they were able. Children as young as 5 learned

to wrap wool yarn around a stick or knead bread, freeing older siblings to do more difficult chores. Young boys used jackknives to carve wood into spoons, bowls, and **trenchers**. Older boys sometimes worked as apprentices, learning trades such as blacksmith, **cooper**, or cobbler from a skilled worker. Girls stayed close to their mothers, learning how to clean and prepare food, care for the animals, and keep their younger siblings busy and quiet.

For the first decades, New England housing was crude. One writer half-jokingly reported that his father, who had arrived in 1630, "was wont to find shelter at night in an empty **cask**."[3] By the end of the century, most New Englanders lived in houses made of wood or stone, or both. Homes were built with **sloped** roofs to allow the winter snow to slide off.

Each village with more than 100 families had a public school. Shivering in one-room schoolhouses, boys learned reading, Latin, and math. Educating girls was not important to many New England parents. As long as their girls could read the Bible, they often viewed further education as a waste of time.

Despite the long hours of work, New Englanders still found time for fun. Picnics and gatherings with other families provided a break from the drudgery of house or farm work. Children jumped rope, played tennis, swung on ropes, and had contests of strength and speed. The whirligig was a favorite toy in New England, easily crafted from a scrap of wood and a piece of string.

The Middle Colonies: Delaware, New Jersey, New York, Pennsylvania

Settlers from all over Europe came to the Middle Colonies. English, Swedes, Dutch, Germans, Scots, Irish, and French

all brought their customs, talents, and religions to the region.

The climate and soil of the Middle Colonies were ideal for growing wheat, barley, and oats, earning these colonies the nickname "the breadbasket colonies." Rivers such as the Hudson and Delaware carried excess crops to other colonies. The colonists also sent some of those valuable grains to England.

Family roles in the Middle Colonies were similar to those in New England. Women cared for the children, managed meals, made clothing, and kept house. Men and older boys worked long hours planting and harvesting, often returning home to chop wood or do other household chores.

There wasn't much time for recreation but that doesn't mean the colonists didn't have fun. Colonists are shown playing a game of bowls, similar to bowling. Most games and sports used very simple equipment as the colonists had to make everything themselves.

Children in the Middle Colonies learned to make candles, gather berries, and help with the animals and the harvest. They often attended church schools rather than public schools. There they were taught the religion of their parents as well as reading and math. Girls generally did not attend school, unless they were Quakers. Quakers believed all children should be educated. For fun, children made puppets, played catch and stickball, and ran races. They skated in the winter and swam in the summer. Country fairs were also a popular pastime.

Many homes in the Middle Colonies were influenced by the styles brought by Dutch settlers. These buildings were tall, narrow, and made of brick. Beds were built into the walls so they didn't take up floor space during the day. Blue and white tiles, like those in Holland, were a favorite decoration around fireplaces.

The Southern Colonies: Maryland, Georgia, North Carolina, South Carolina, Virginia

In every colony, some people had more money or land than others. Those who had more lived a relatively easier life than their neighbors who had less. Nowhere was this more true than in the South.

Although Maryland was originally settled as a religious colony, southern colonists were generally more interested in wealth than religion. Some farmers owned very large farms called plantations, where they grew crops like cotton, rice, or tobacco. Plantations varied in size from 125 to 1000 acres, or even more.

Most plantations were self-sufficient, providing everything from food to clothes to furniture for the people who lived on the property. For this reason, southern colonists didn't have much need for town centers or shops.

Large numbers of "hands," usually slaves or indentured servants, were required for plantations to be efficient and profitable. Slaves were owned by plantation masters and not paid for their labor. Indentured servants, most of them male, had the cost of their voyage from Europe paid by a wealthy person. Indentured servants spent at least five years working to pay off the price of their passage. One tobacco planter summed it up when he wrote, "If a man has Money, Negroes and Land enough, he is a complete Gentleman."[4] The wives of these "Gentlemen" stayed busy managing the household, supervising meals, and caring for their often large families and many guests.

The homes of the wealthy were filled with tapestries, rugs, paintings, clocks, imported furniture, and books. They made time for hunting, playing cards, and visiting other plantations. Because their properties were so far apart, plantation life could be lonely.

Before farmers could plant crops, they had to clear the land. This backbreaking work took a long time and required the help of every able-bodied male. These South Carolina colonists may be planting beans, pumpkins, onions, or corn.

The colonists usually dressed as they had in England and Europe. Boys and girls generally wore a simple cotton dress until they reached the age of 6 or 7. After that, they dressed like adults.

Southerners believed that education was the responsibility of the family, not the community. Children of the rich were taught by private tutors. The boys studied in the fall and helped in the fields during the spring and summer. Girls were not always educated. When they were, they studied during the summer so they could weave and help around the house during the winter. Twenty-year-old Eliza Lucas Pinckney described her daily life in her South Carolina plantation in a letter to a friend:

> In general then I rise at five o'Clock in the morning, read till Seven, then take a walk in the garden or field, see that the Servants [slaves] are at their respective business [working], then to breakfast. The first hour after breakfast is spent at my musick, the next is constantly employed in recolecting [studying or practicing] something I have learned lest for want of practise it should be quite lost [something I have not studied enough and might forget if I don't practice], such as French and short hand. After that I devote the rest of the time till I dress for dinner to our little Polly and two black girls who I teach to read.[5]

The majority of southerners worked much smaller farms, typically about 100 acres. They raised livestock and grew crops such as corn, wheat, barley, and oats. These families managed with crude housing, basic clothing, and simple furniture. Both men and women hunted, farmed, and cared for their families. Children on smaller farms were often not educated or were taught by their parents to read and do simple arithmetic.

Tituba, a female slave owned by Salem minister Samuel Parris, was accused of practicing voodoo and witchcraft in 1692. This accusation set off the Salem Witch Trials. Tituba was imprisoned and eventually released. Others weren't so fortunate. Nineteen people were hanged and one man was pressed to death with heavy stones.

Religion and Holidays

Religion, particularly Christianity, played a central role in the lives of many colonists. As settlers with varied religions and traditions came to America throughout the 17th and 18th centuries, they were forced to rethink the role of religion in their lives and their government.

Just as religious practices varied from colony to colony so, too, did holidays and special events. Weddings, engagements, and baptisms were joyous events, although the celebrations were more often solemn than in modern times. For example, at about age 7, when a boy had survived the most dangerous years for childhood death, families often celebrated his "breeching." He began wearing breeches (long pants). The end of a young man's apprenticeship—his training to learn a trade—was also marked by gifts of new clothes and perhaps a set of tools to use in his new profession.

Although the colonists observed many holidays we have long since forgotten, most celebrated Christmas and New Year's. Some of the holiday traditions the settlers brought from their home countries are woven into our present-day celebrations.

CHAPTER 3

New England Colonies

The Massachusetts Puritans believed their form of Protestantism was God's true religion. Although they came to the New World to practice their religion freely, they did not allow others to do the same. Rhode Island and Connecticut, both founded in 1636, were started by men who were **exiled** from Massachusetts because they would not follow the strict Puritan rules. Two years later, Exeter, one of the first towns in New Hampshire, was founded by another Massachusetts exile. He had dared to defend a woman who spoke out against the Puritans.

Puritans lived by a rigid moral code. Behaviors outside their code, from dozing in church to stealing food, were harshly punished. They also believed God punished sinful behavior by bringing sickness upon a family, or a poor crop to an unfaithful community.

Fear of the devil was common in New England. Puritans believed **Satan** chose women, children, and the insane to carry out his work. Those who followed Satan were considered witches. The Salem Witch Trials of 1692 were an example of the extremes the Puritans went to in ridding their community of the devil. The trials lasted for three months. When they ended, 20 people accused of witchcraft had been executed.

By 1750, there were 18 churches in the city of Boston alone.[1] Residents who failed to attend worship services on Sunday morning and afternoon were fined or put into **stocks**. Those bold enough to speak out against the church could be whipped or have small slices of their ears cut off. More serious offenses were punished with exile from the community, or even hanging.

The people of Rhode Island disagreed with the strict Puritan rules and invited people of all religions to their colony. It was the first colony to openly welcome Jews. The first synagogue in America, the Touro Synagogue, was dedicated in 1763 in Newport. The disapproving Puritans called Rhode Island "the **latrine** of New England" because it had no religious requirements for citizenship.[2]

New England Holy Days

"They for whom all days are holy can have no holidays."[3] This popular 17th century saying summed up the Puritan attitude about holidays. Any holiday not mentioned in the Bible was not celebrated. Christmas was banned in Massachusetts from 1659 to 1681, and even the sale of plum pudding was forbidden. The Puritans also did not celebrate Easter, Valentine's Day, or Michaelmas, a holiday usually observed on February 2nd.

The main Puritan holiday was the Sabbath, observed every Sunday. They also observed days of fasting when conditions were going badly for the community and they thought God was punishing them. Days of thanksgiving were declared when things were going well and they believed God was pleased.

The first Thanksgiving dates back to the fall of 1621, and was shared by the settlers and Wampanoag Indians. The three-day feast included **venison**, duck, seafood, corn, squash, bread, green vegetables, and berries. Connecticut celebrated a thanksgiving in 1639. Feast days occurred more regularly after 1660.

The Middle Colonies

From 1626 through the mid-1700s, Quakers, Methodists, Mennonites, Lutherans, Dutch Calvinists, Presbyterians, Jews, and others flocked to the middle colonies. By 1701, New Jersey alone had 45 distinct congregations![4] Each

group brought its homeland holidays and traditions. Native Americans and slaves, with religious traditions of their own, added more variety to the patchwork of religion in the Middle Colonies.

Religious tolerance for all Christian **denominations** was the law in the Middle Colonies but not always the reality. For example, Presbyterians argued that Quakers should not serve in the government since they showed "more real Affection for Enemy Savages [referring to black slaves and Indians] than for their fellow Subjects, of certain Denominations."[5] In New York, Quakers and Jews were not allowed to vote in at least two elections. In time, however, these diverse groups learned to live together. As one writer observed in 1782, "the strict modes of Christianity as practised in Europe are lost. . . . Here individuals of all nations (and religions) are melted into a new race."[6]

Sinterklaas and Other Middle Colony Traditions

It was in the Middle Colonies that Christmas developed as a holiday. During the 17th and 18th centuries, it was a rowdy celebration with drinking and public celebration. Small gifts of money, little books, or sweets were sometimes given to children by their parents at Christmas or New Years.

The Dutch settlers of New York brought many holiday traditions with them. At Christmas, parents filled wooden shoes with fruit and candy for their children. Sinterklaas, or Santa Claus, was also introduced by the Dutch in the early 1700s and melded over time with St. Nicholas, the British Father Christmas, and other mid-winter gift bearers. Although Easter was not widely celebrated in the colonies, the Dutch began the tradition of dying eggs. Pinkster, or Pentecost, was also observed by the Dutch as a time for

families to come together and celebrate baptisms, confirmations, and the coming of spring. On First Skating Day, a Dutch tradition celebrating the first day that ponds froze, children and adults spent the day skating with friends and family.

Many Christian religions have a winter gift-giver in their Christmas traditions. He may go by the name St. Nicholas, Father Christmas, Sinterklaas, Santa Claus, or the Lord of Christmas. This print shows St. Nicholas with an evergreen bough (a symbol of everlasting life) and a basket which may contain gifts for children.

There were other uniquely Middle Colony holidays. Although New Year's Eve was not generally celebrated, Watch Night, practiced in Philadelphia by the Methodists in the mid-1700s, was a quiet way to reflect about the past year and the one to come. German settlers brought their traditions for Candlemas. Celebrated on February 2nd, farmers predicted if spring would come early or winter would linger. It was an early version of Groundhog Day.[7]

The Southern Colonies

During the 17th and 18th centuries, Roman Catholics, Huguenots, German Pietists, Moravians, Quakers, Baptists, and Presbyterians lived together in the Southern Colonies. This sparsely populated region welcomed all Christian settlers willing to defend the land and build the economy.

Many of the people living there were African slaves. Slaves were usually non-Christian, and colonists felt free to enslave Africans who were not Christians. From the beginning of colonial slavery in the south until the early 18th century, laws made it illegal to baptize slaves. Owners believed that if their slaves became Christian, they would have to set them free.[8]

As more settlers came to the south, they practiced their Old World beliefs and traditions and passed them down to their children. Although disputes and violence did occur among the different groups, religious pluralism (the policy of many religions co-existing in society) was generally accepted as the key to peace and economic prosperity.

A Southern Christmas

Christmas was celebrated in the South as both a religious holiday and the start of a season of joy and merrymaking.

Feasts, fireworks, visiting friends, dances, parties, and hunting all began on Christmas before an enormous blazing Yule log. This custom, which the colonists brought from England, involved water-soaking a large log. The festivities continued as long as the Yule log burned. Another tradition was to save the last bit of the current year's log to kindle the log the following year.

Homes were decorated with fragrant greenery such as holly, pine, cedar, laurels, magnolia, and mistletoe. Southerners wove wreaths, lit large Christmas candles, and burned incense.

Good smells also came from southern kitchens during the Christmas season. Traditions varied from house to house, but a large plantation Christmas dinner could take weeks to prepare. The menu might include at least seven types of meat, brown and white breads, potatoes, parsnips, fruit, traditional sweets from the family's homeland, and a grand Christmas pie. The recipe for this special "pie" called for a turkey stuffed with goose, chicken, pigeon, and seasonings and sealed inside a heavy crust.[9]

"Father Christmas," also called the "The Lord of Christmas," was a central figure in the celebration. But the Southern Santa looked nothing like "the dapper little Manhattan goblin called Santa Claus."[10] Father Christmas was plump and regal, with a beard and long hair of Spanish moss. This Santa carried mistletoe in one hand and delivered gifts to children with the other. Slaves and servants also often received clothes, extra food, or small gifts from their masters at Christmastime.

Colonists and Indians benefited from the fur trade. Here, white settlers and Native Americans talk and play with each others' children on a trading day.

If Your Skin Wasn't White

How you lived in the 13 colonies generally depended on when you lived and which colony you lived in. The life of a Rhode Island Quaker in 1640 was much different than the life of a poor Georgian farmer in 1740. But there was another factor that determined how you lived in colonial days: the color of your skin.

Long before the first European colonists arrived in 1607, the coast of North America was inhabited by native people who had lived on the land for hundreds of years. Over 100 years before Jamestown, Christopher Columbus called these people "Indians," in his mistaken belief that he had landed in India. Many Indians lived within the boundaries of the 13 colonies. The relationship between natives and colonists was sometimes peaceful and **amicable** but often violent and destructive.

Many settlers saw the advantages of good relations with the native people. Besides avoiding the dangers of attack, the early settlers faced life and death challenges with food and shelter. The Native Americans taught them to hunt and plant crops in an unfamiliar land.

Mutual Benefits

In many cases, the natives and the colonists entered into trade that benefited both sides. The Indians had animal furs and hides which the colonists made into **muffs** and hats or sent back to England to sell. The colonists had metal tools like hoes, axes, and knives, as well as manufactured cloth. These items made life easier for the native people but it also changed their traditional ways of farming, hunting, and clothing themselves.

Many Indians were initially trusting of the European newcomers. But their trust quickly faded when the settlers did not return their generosity and respect. As early as 1609, Powhatan, the leader of more than 30 tribes in the area of the Jamestown settlement, witnessed the white man's disrespect for Indian traditions, culture, and religion. Surprised by the colonists' unfriendly ways, he said,

> Why should you take by force that which you can have by love? Why should you destroy us, who have provided you with food?. . . . You see us unarmed, and willing to supply your wants, if you will come in a friendly manner, and not with swords and guns.[1]

Despite their dependence on the Indians, most whites believed them to be an inferior race—childlike, simple, ignorant, and uncivilized. Many settlers felt entitled to claim the Indians' lands for themselves and teach the native people the "right" way to live.

The Puritans of New England and the Quakers of the Middle Colonies in particular considered it their moral and religious duty to forcibly convert the native population to Christianity. They described the Indians as "hopeless, vicious, and undeserving."[2] They believed the native people

were savages. This attitude justified their disrespect for Indian religions.

The Indians faced other challenges as well. The white men had guns, swords, and cannons, far more than the Indians could protect themselves against. The settlers also brought germs and disease. Most Europeans were able to fight off the germs they carried because they had been exposed to them for generations. But diseases such as smallpox and influenza killed up to 70 percent of some native populations.[3] The high death rate devastated Indian societies and disrupted the passing down of traditions from one generation to the next.

Within a short time after establishing their settlements, colonists pushed into native lands and claimed it for themselves. They felled the precious forests which provided the Indians with timber and plants for food and medicine. They killed wild game and disrupted the native peoples' way of living.

Conflicts Break Out

The Indians did not simply accept the intrusion of the white man. Fierce wars were fought between the Indians and the settlers throughout the 13 colonies. One of the worst was King Philip's War (1675–76) between Massachusetts colonists and the Wampanoag tribe. This bloody war claimed the lives of one in 10 combatants on both sides, and resulted in the burning of critical food stores and 1,200 colonists' homes.[4]

American Indians were also sometimes captured and enslaved by the colonists. Some scholars estimate the numbers to be in the tens of thousands.[5] Most were shipped to Barbados, Bermuda, Jamaica, the Azores, Spain, and Tangier in North Africa, although some were forced to work the farms of the northern colonies or southern plantations.

The African Slaves

By the time of the American Revolution in 1776, one in five people living in the 13 colonies had very dark, or "black" skin.[6] Most were slaves, who were brought to the colonies under the most inhumane circumstances. Violently stolen from their villages in West Africa, the captives were exchanged to **slavers** for rum, guns, gunpowder, textiles, or trinkets. Slavers crammed their new "property" below the decks of ships.

As many as 40 percent of the captives did not live through the infamous "Middle Passage," the three-month sail from Africa to the Caribbean or the American colonies. Slavers traded those who survived for sugar and molasses, which they used to make more rum.

Although people usually think only of the Southern Colonies in black slavery, all 13 colonies were deeply involved in the slave trade. During a trip from her home in Boston to New York City in 1704, Sarah Kemble Knight commented disapprovingly about what she regarded as the lenient treatment of slaves in Connecticut:

> Too Indulgent [are] (especially ye [the] farmers) to their slaves: sufering [allowing] too great familiarity from them, permitting ym [them] to sit at Table and eat with them, (as they say to save time,) and into the dish goes the black hoof as freely as the white hand."[7]

Clearly, Knight saw Africans as less human than whites, comparing their hands to the feet of animals. Many of her fellow colonists shared her low opinion.

"A Loathsome Stench"

Olaudah Equiano

Few personal accounts by slaves who lived during colonial times have survived. One significant exception was Olaudah Equiano, a man born in southern Nigeria in 1745 and taken from his village at the age of 10. He described the "loathsomeness of the stench" of the voyage from Africa, caused by hundreds of men, women and children chained below decks with no air, no place to relieve themselves, and barely enough space to turn around. Seasick and terrified about their futures, many slaves could not stomach the **putrid** food they were forced to eat. Equiano wrote:

> on my refusing to eat, one of (the slavers) held me fast by the hands, and . . . tied my feet, while the other **flogged** me severely. . . . I would have jumped over the side, but I could not; and besides, the crew used to watch us very closely who were not chained down to the decks, lest we should leap into the water; and I have seen some of these poor African prisoners most severely cut for attempting to do so, and hourly whipped for not eating. This indeed was often the case with myself.[8]

Once the slaves arrived at their destination, "masters" bid for them at auction, paying the highest price for men who looked strong and healthy. If a slave had scars from a whip, a master might think the slave was rebellious or disobedient, and would offer a lower price.

Slaves labored from dawn to dusk six days a week with little or no hope of ever being free. Their specific jobs were

Charleſtown, July 24th, 1769.

TO BE SOLD,

On THURSDAY the third Day of AUGUST next,

A CARGO OF NINETY-FOUR PRIME, HEALTHY

NEGROES,

CONSISTING OF

Thirty-nine MEN, Fifteen BOYS, Twenty-four WOMEN, and Sixteen GIRLS.

JUST ARRIVED,

In the Brigantine DEMBIA, *Francis Bare*, Maſter, from SIERRA-LEON, by

DAVID & JOHN DEAS.

This print from the colony of New York in the 1700s shows a well-dressed slave working in a private home. The inset advertisement for a slave auction in 1769 is a reminder that even this seemingly content African was considered property that could be bought or sold at his master's whim.

determined by whether they lived in a town, on a plantation, or a farm. Many slaves were separated from their families and grieved the loss of their loved ones for decades. Slaves were not permitted to practice their cultural traditions or religious beliefs.

Property, Not People

Africans were considered to be property, not people, and were often treated in the harshest manner. Each colony passed special laws, called slaves codes, to control their slaves and prevent rebellions. The specific laws varied from colony to colony.

In most colonies, it was illegal for anyone besides the owner to provide food, shelter, or transportation out of the colony to a slave. Slaves were forbidden to read or write. They were often forced to change their names from their African names to new ones chosen by their owners. They could be searched at any time and masters could sell the children of slaves away from their parents. Slaves were forbidden to carry a stick or a cane, or to walk on the streets at night or on Sundays. Slave women were often the victims of sexual violence by their owners, who were completely protected by the codes. Marriage among slaves always required the approval of the master.

It was not until 1783 that New England and the Middle Colonies started to pass laws against the enslavement of blacks. The laws were written to gradually allow slaves more freedom over time. But the Southern Colonies did not want to give up their slaves. Their economy depended on the free labor of millions of black people to work their **elaborate** plantations. It would take the Civil War to get the South to finally free their slaves.

Festivals were times when hard-working settlers could mingle, share news, and relax. A liberty pole, an ancient symbol of freedom, is being raised. The inset shows several men pulling down a sign with the likeness of King George III on it.

5

How Things Change!

Most of the early settlers who landed in Massachusetts, Virginia, and Maryland considered themselves British citizens. Until the mid-1700s, they were happy to have British support as they built new homes, grew their businesses, worked their farms, and raised their families. Throughout the generations, however, the new Americans had grown self-sufficient and proud of the colonies they had established.

By 1775, Massachusetts had grown from a handful of Pilgrims to a thriving colony with vibrant towns and villages, five newspapers, and the best school system in the colonies. The ports in Boston and Salem were busy with trading ships from around the world.

Jamestown, which had all but been starved out of existence in 1607, was covered with wheat and corn fields and tobacco plantations. The larger Virginia colony had expanded to include modern-day West Virginia and Kentucky, and claimed territory northwest of the Ohio River.[1]

Maryland, which had begun as a haven for Catholics, was home to large communities of Quakers, Lutherans, the Church of England, and other religions. By the 1750s, the colony not only grew tobacco, wheat, and corn but also had a thriving iron industry and exported thousands of tons of iron to England each year.[2]

Changing Relationship

The relationship between the colonies and Mother England had changed over the years. Many of the newer colonists did not feel the same loyalty and respect for King George III, who assumed the throne in 1760, as their great-great-grand-parents had for his predecessors. In addition, the British victory in the French and Indian War (1754–63) had made living conditions safer for many colonists but was very expensive. King George and Parliament (the British governing body) believed the colonies should bear some of the financial burden.

Parliament began imposing taxes and restrictions on the colonists. It became more expensive for them to earn a living and trade **goods** with other countries. The Sugar Act of 1764 taxed molasses, used for making rum. It also strictly enforced rules against smuggling, which the colonists had been doing for decades to get around the high cost of British goods. The Stamp Act of 1765 added an extra cost to anything that required the use of paper, such as legal documents, newspapers, books, and playing cards. The 1767 Townsend Duties taxed several imports. Other taxes also took power away from the colonies.

The colonists began to protest and **boycott** English products. The boycotts hurt the British economy and Parliament eventually repealed (did away with) many of the taxes.

Power to the People

These repeals made the colonists realize they had power against England if they stood together. Men like James Otis, Jr, of Massachusetts and John Dickinson of Pennsylvania wrote widely distributed pamphlets insisting that Parliament shouldn't tax them because their voices were not represented there.

Despite the repeals, some taxes remained. Tensions continued to escalate. In December, 1773, men disguised as Indians threw hundreds of chests of tea into Boston Harbor. The king and Parliament were furious. They cracked down on the city. The following September, the First Continental Congress met in Philadelphia. Representatives from the colonies discussed the best ways of responding to what they saw as continuing injustices from the British. They also sent a petition to King George that explained their **grievances**. The king ignored it.

In March, 1775, Patrick Henry, one of Virginia's great patriots, wrote "I know not what course others may take, but as for me, give me liberty or give me death!"[3] The following month, battles between colonists and British troops broke out in the Massachusetts towns of Lexington and Concord. A revolution was brewing.

In July, 1776, the colonists declared their independence. The ensuing Revolutionary War lasted until 1783. At that point, the 13 colonies ceased to exist. In their place, the United States of America arose from the battlefield. A new country had begun.

APPENDIX

ORIGINAL SOURCE DOCUMENTS

National Humanities Center, Eliza Lucas Pinckney, Letters & Memoranda, 1740–1762.

Sayer, A New Map of North America, ca. 1750, detail

"I find it requires great care, attention and activity to attend properly to a Carolina Estate."

Eliza Lucas Pinckney

Letters & Memoranda, 1740-1762

Eliza Lucas Pinckney (ca. 1722-1793) is renowned for introducing the cultivation of indigo for dye to the American colonies. Born in the West Indies where her father, a British army officer, was based, she was educated in England and moved with her family to South Carolina in 1738. As a teenager she managed her father's plantation while he was away and, years later, managed her husband's plantation after his death. Her rich letters and memoranda reveal her autonomy, perseverance, and downright grit as she forged an unique life for an elite colonial woman.

May 2, 1740__letter to her friend Mrs. Boddicott in England ***Age 18***

I flatter myself it will be a satisfaction to you to hear I like this part of the world, as my lott has fallen here — which I really do. I prefer England to it, 'tis true, but think Carolina greatly preferable to the West Indias, and was my Papa here I should be very happy.

We have a very good acquaintance from whom we have received much friendship and Civility. Charles Town, the principal one in this province, is a polite, agreeable place. The people live very Gentile and very much in the English taste. The Country is in General fertile and abounds with Venison and wild fowl; the Venison is much higher flavoured than in England but 'tis seldom fatt.

My Papa and Mama's great indulgence to me leaves it to me to chose our place of residence either in town or Country,[1] but I think it more prudent as well as most agreeable to my Mama and self to be in the Country during my Father's absence. We are 17 mile by land and 6 by water from Charles Town — where we have about 6 agreeable families around us with whom we live in great harmony.

I have a little library well furnished (for my papa has left me most of his books) in which I spend part of my time. My Musick and the Garden, which I am very fond of, take up the rest of my time that is not imployed in business, of which my father has left me a pretty good share — and indeed, 'twas inavoidable as my Mama's bad state of health prevents her going through any fatigue.

I have the business of 3 plantations to transact, which requires much writing and more business and fatigue of other sorts than you can imagine. But least you should imagine it too burthensom to a girl at my early time of life, give me leave to answer you: I assure you I think myself happy that I can be useful to so good a father, and by rising very early I find I can go through much business. But least you should think I shall be quite moaped with this way of life I am to inform you there is two worthy Ladies in Charles Town, Mrs. Pinckney[2] and Mrs. Cleland, who are partial enough to me to be always pleased to have me with them, and insist upon my making their houses my home when in town and press me to relax a little much oftener than 'tis in my honor to accept of their obliging intreaties. But I some times am with one or the other for 3 weeks or a month at a time, and then enjoy all the pleasures Charles Town affords, but nothing gives me more than subscribing my self

Dear Madam,
Yr. most affectionet and most obliged humble Servt.
Eliza. Lucas

National Humanities Center, 2008: nationalhumanitiescenter.org/pds. Selections from *The Letterbook of Eliza Lucas Pinckney, 1739-1762*, ed. Elise Pinckney (University of North Carolina Press, 1972); reproduced by permission of the South Carolina Historical Society. Ages approximate due to uncertain birthdate of Eliza Lucas. Footnotes based on information in Elise Pinckney edition; if presented verbatim, page numbers included. Complete image credits at nationalhumanitiescenter.org/pds/ becomingamer/imagecredits.htm.

[1] Colonel Lucas owned property in Charleston as well as his nearby plantation.

[2] Elizabeth Lamb Pinckney, the first wife of Charles Pinckney, died in 1744. Eliza Lucas married Pinckney the following spring.

http://nationalhumanitiescenter.org/pds/becomingamer/peoples/text5/elizapinckney.pdf

National Humanities Center, Travel Journal of Sarah Kemble Knight, 1704–1705, selections on Connecticut.

Sarah Kemble Knight

Remarks on "this whole Colony of Connecticut"

1704-1705

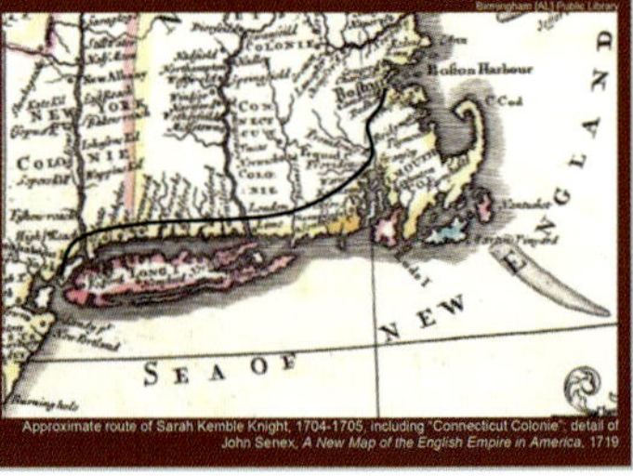

Approximate route of Sarah Kemble Knight, 1704-1705, including "Connecticut Colonie"; detail of John Senex, *A New Map of the English Empire in America*, 1719

In contrast to the homogenous colony of Massachusetts Bay, other northern colonies such as Connecticut, New York, and Pennsylvania became more diverse as German, Scot, Irish, Dutch, and French immigrants arrived by the thousands — a development often noted in colonists" diaries and travel journals. In October 1704, a Boston widow named Sarah Kemble Knight began a five-month round-trip journey to New York City to complete some family business after a cousin's death. She travelled alone, staying in inns along the route, and employing local men as guides. In these excerpts from her travel journal in which she combines observation and satire (and which she later read aloud at a women's literary "tea-table" which she hosted), Knight describes the colony of Connecticut, emphasizing the diversity and prosperity of its white inhabitants: "No one that can and will be diligent in this place need fear poverty, nor the want of food and raiment."

SATURDAY, OCT. 7TH [1704], we set out early in the Morning, and being something unacquainted with the way, having asked it of some we met, they told us we must Ride a mile or two and turn down a Lane on the Right hand; and by their Direction we Rode on, but not That coming to the turning, we met a Young fellow and asked him how far it was to the Lane which turn'd down towards Guilford [Connecticut]. He said we must Ride a little further, and turn down by the Corner of uncle Sam's Lot. My Guide vented his Spleen at the Lubber; and we soon after came into the Road, and keeping still on, without anything further Remarkable, about two o'clock afternoon we arrived at New Haven, where I was received with all Possible Respects and civility. Here I discharged Mr. Wheeler with a reward to his satisfaction, and took some time to rest after so long and toilsome a journey; And Inform'd myself of the manners and customs of the place, and at the same time employed myself in the affair I went there upon.

They are Govern'd by the same Laws as we in Boston (or little differing) throughout this whole Colony of Connecticut, And much the same way of Church Government, and many of them good, Sociable people, and I hope Religious too: but a little too much Independent in their principles, and, as I have been told, were formerly in their Zeal very Rigid in their Administrations towards such as their Laws made Offenders, even to a harmless Kiss or Innocent merriment among Young people. Whipping being a frequent and counted an easy Punishment, about which as other Crimes, the Judges were absolute in their Sentences. They told me a pleasant story about a pair of Justices in those parts, which I may not omit the relation of.

A negro Slave belonging to a man in the Town stole a hogshead [wooden barrel] from his master, and

National Humanities Center, 2008: nationalhumanitiescenter.org/pds/. First published in 1825 as *The Journal of Madam Knight*, ed. Thomas Dwight. Spelling and punctuation modernized, and bracketed annotations added, by NHC for clarity. Complete image credits at nationalhumanitiescenter.org/pds/becomingamer/imagecredits.htm.

http://nationalhumanitiescenter.org/pds/becomingamer/growth/text1/connecticutknight.pdf

APPENDIX

ORIGINAL SOURCE DOCUMENTS

Black Founders: The Free Black Community in the Early Republic

THE
INTERESTING NARRATIVE
OF
THE LIFE
OF
OLAUDAH EQUIANO,
OR
GUSTAVUS VASSA,
THE AFRICAN.
WRITTEN BY HIMSELF.

VOL. I.

Behold, God is my ſalvation : I will truſt and not be afraid, for the Lord Jehovah is my ſtrength and my ſong : he alſo is become my ſalvation.
And in that day ſhall ye ſay, Praiſe the Lord, call upon his name, declare his doings among the people.
Iſaiah xii. 2, 4.

FIRST AMERICAN EDITION.

NEW-YORK:
PRINTED and Sold BY W. DURELL, *at his Book-Store and Printing-Office*, No. 19, Q. Street.
M,DCC,XCI.

http://www.librarycompany.org/blackfounders/section3.htm

Higginson, Francis. *New-England's Plantation.* London, England: T.C. and R.C. for Michael Sparke, 1630.

New-Englands Plantation

there are some of the lesser sort, they tell me, that by a certaine Skill will fly from Tree to Tree though they stand farre distant.

Of the Waters of New-England, *with the things belonging to the same.*

New-England hath Water enough both salt and fresh, the greatest Sea in the World, the *Atlanticke* Sea runs all along the Coast thereof. There are abundance of Ilands along the Shore, some full of Wood and Mast to feed Swine; and others cleere of Wood, and fruitfull to beare Corne. Also wee haue store of excellent harbours for Ships, as at Cape *Anne*, and at *Masathulets* Bay, and at *Salem*, and at many other places: and they are the better because for Strangers there is a verie difficult and dangerous passage into them, but vnto such as are well acquainted with them, they are easie and safe enough. The aboundance of Sea-Fish are almost beyond beleeuing, and sure I should scarce haue beleeued it, except I had seene it with mine owne Eyes. I saw great store of Whales, and Crampusse, and such aboundance of Mackerils that it would astonish one to behold, likewise Cod-Fish in aboundance

[96] on

https://archive.org/stream/newenglandsplant00higgrich#page/96/mode/2up

CHAPTER NOTES

Chapter 1: A New Beginning

1. "Jamestown Settlement and the 'Starving Time.'" http://www.ushistory.org/us/2c.asp

2. "Context and Developments: The Pilgrims." http://xroads.virginia.edu/~CAP/PURITAN/purhist.html

3. Roberta Wiener and James Arnold. *Maryland: The History of Maryland Colony, 1634–1776* (Chicago: Raintree, 2005), p. 14.

4. Ibid. p. 24.

Chapter 2: Everyday Life

1. "Benjamin Franklin FAQ." https://www.fi.edu/benjamin-franklin-faq

2. Francis Higginson, *New-Englands Plantation with The Sea Journal and Other Writings* (Salem, MA: Essex Book and Print Club, 1908), p. 97. https://archive.org/details/newenglandsplantoohiggrich

3. George Francis Dow, *Everyday Life in the Massachusetts Bay Colony* (Mineola, NY: Dover Publications, 1988), p. 16.

4. James Lawrence, *The Rise and fall of the British Empire* (New York: St. Martins Press, 1994), p. 40.

5. Eliza Lucas Pinckney, "Eliza Lucas Pinckney: Letters & Memoranda, 1740–1762." National Humanities Center. http://nationalhumanitiescenter.org/pds/becomingamer/peoples/text5/elizapinckney.pdf

Chapter 3: Religion and Holidays

1. "Religion in Colonial America: Trends, Regulations and Beliefs." https://www.facinghistory.org/nobigotry/religion-colonial-america-trends-regulations-and-beliefs

2. Cassandra Niemczyk. "The American Puritans: Did You Know? Little-known or remarkable facts about the American Puritans." http://www.christianitytoday.com/history/issues/issue-41/american-puritans-did-you-know.html

3. "Puritan Easter or The Devil's Holiday." http://www.newenglandhistoricalsociety.com/puritan-easter-devils-holiday/

4. Patricia Bonomi, "Religious Pluralism in the Middle Colonies." http://nationalhumanitiescenter.org/tserve/eighteen/ekeyinfo/midcol.htm

5. Ibid.

6. Ibid.

7. Russell Roberts, *Holidays and Celebrations in Colonial America* (Hockessin, DE: Mitchell Lane Publishers, 2007), pp. 19–23.

8. "Religion in the Colonies, Southern Colonies." http://countriesquest.com/north_america/usa/people/religion_in_the_united_states/history_of_religion_in_the_united_states/religion_in_the_colonies/southern_colonies.htm

9. J.O. Bledsoe "Christmas in the Early South." Know Southern History.net. http://www.knowsouthernhistory.net/Articles/History/Prior%201850/christmas_in_early_south.html

10. Ibid.

Chapter 4: If Your Skin Wasn't White

1. Karin Coddon, editor. *Colonial America* (Farmington Hills, MI: Greenhaven Press, 2003), pp. 78-79.

2. Don Nardo, *Early Native North Americans* (Detroit: Lucent Books, 2008), p. 91.

3. "Changes in American Indian Life." https://www.boundless.com/u-s-history/textbooks/boundless-u-s-history-textbook/expansion-of-the-colonies-1650-1750-4/early-conflicts-49/changes-in-american-indian-life-1354-10438/

4. Mike Messina, "America's Most Devastating Conflict: King Philip's War." https://connecticuthistory.org/americas-most-devastating-conflict-king-philips-war/

5. "Changes in American Indian Life."

6. Rosemarie Zagarri. "Slavery in Colonial British North America." http://teachinghistory.org/history-content/ask-a-historian/25577

7. Sarah Kemble Knight, *The Journal of Madam Knight* (Bedford, MA: Applewood Books, 1992), p. 38.

8. Olaudah Equiano, "Personal account of an enslaved African." http://www.discoveringbristol.org.uk/slavery/routes/from-africa-to-america/ship-journals/enslaved-african-account/

Chapter 5: How Things Change!

1. Warren Hofstra, "Backcountry Frontier of Colonial Virginia." https://www.encyclopediavirginia.org/Backcountry_Frontier_of_Colonial_Virginia#start_entry

2. Roberta Wiener and James Arnold, Maryland, *The History of Maryland Colony, 1634–1776* (Chicago: Raintree, 2005), pp. 46–47.

3. Debra Kent, *Virginia* (New York: Scholastic, 2010), p. 43.

FURTHER READING

Day, Nancy. *Your Travel Guide to Colonial America*. Minneapolis, MN: Runestone Press, 2001.

Isaacs, Sally Senzell. *Colonists and Independence*. New York: Kingfisher, 2011.

McCarthy, Pat. *The 13 Colonies from Founding to Revolution in American History*. Berkeley Heights, NJ: Enslow,2004.

Nobleman, Marc Tyler. *The Thirteen Colonies*. Minneapolis, MN: Compass Point Books, 2002.

Worth, Richard. *Colonial America: Building Toward Independence*. Berkeley Heights, NJ: Enslow, 2006.

WORKS CONSULTED

"America a Christian Nation." Sites Google.com. https://sites.google.com/site/americachristiannation/

"Benjamin Franklin FAQ." Franklin Institute.edu. https://www.fi.edu/benjamin-franklin-faq

Bledsoe, J.O. "Christmas in the Early South." Know Southern History.net. http://www.knowsouthernhistory.net/Articles/History/Prior%201850/christmas_in_early_south.html

Bonomi, Patricia. "Religious Pluralism in the Middle Colonies." National Humanities Center.org. http://nationalhumanitiescenter.org/tserve/eighteen/ekeyinfo/midcol.htm

"Changes in American Indian Life." Boundless.com. https://www.boundless.com/u-s-history/textbooks/boundless-u-s-history-textbook/expansion-of-the-colonies-1650-1750-4/early-conflicts-49/changes-in-american-indian-life-1354-10438/

Coddon, Karin, Ed. *Colonial America*. Farmington Hills: Greenhaven Press, 2003.

Coughtry, Jay. "The Notorious Triangle." Cyberspace.com. http://www.cyberspace.org/jh/egh/coughtry.html

Dow, George Francis. *Everyday Life in the Massachusetts Bay Colony*. Mineola, NY: Dover Publications, 1988.

Equiano, Olaudah. "Personal Account of an Enslaved African." Discovering Bristol.org. http://www.discoveringbristol.org.uk/slavery/routes/from-africa-to-america/ship-journals/enslaved-african-account/

Harper, Douglas. "Slavery in the North." http://slavenorth.com/index.html.

Higginson, Francis. *New-Englands Plantation with The Sea Journal and Other Writings*. Salem, MA: Essex Book and Print Club, 1908. https://archive.org/details/newenglandsplantoohiggrich

Hofstra, Warren. "Backcountry Frontier of Colonial Virginia." Encyclopedia Virginia.org. https://www.encyclopediavirginia.org/Backcountry_Frontier_of_Colonial_Virginia#start_entry

Kent, Debra. *Virginia*. New York: Scholastic, 2010.

WORKS CONSULTED

Knight, Sarah Kemble. *The Journal of Madam Knight*. Bedford, MA: Applewood Books, 1992.

Lawrence, James. *The Rise and Fall of the British Empire*. New York: St. Martins Press, 1994.

Messina, Mike. "America's Most Devastating Conflict: King Philip's War." Connecticut History.org. https://connecticuthistory.org/americas-most-devastating-conflict-king-philips-war/

Nardo. Don. *Early Native North Americans*. Detroit: Lucent Books, 2008.

Niemczyk, Cassandra. "The American Puritans: Did You Know? Little-known or remarkable facts about the American Puritans." Christianity Today.com. http://www.christianitytoday.com/history/issues/issue-41/american-puritans-did-you-know.html

"Puritan Easter or The Devil's Holiday." New England Historical Society.com. http://www.newenglandhistoricalsociety.com/puritan-easter-devils-holiday/

Sayles, Jameka. "Child Life in the New England Colonies." Teacher Institute Yale.edu. http://teachersinstitute.yale.edu/curriculum/units/2003/2/03.02.06.x.html

"Religion in Colonial America: Trends, Regulations and Beliefs." Facing History.org. https://www.facinghistory.org/nobigotry/religion-colonial-america-trends-regulations-and-beliefs

"Religion in the Colonies, Southern Colonies." Countries Quest.com. http://countriesquest.com/north_america/usa/people/religion_in_the_united_states/history_of_religion_in_the_united_states/religion_in_the_colonies/southern_colonies.htm

Roberts, Russell. *Holidays and Celebrations in Colonial America*. Hockessin, DE: Mitchell Lane Publishers, 2007.

Wiener, Roberta and Arnold, James. *Maryland, The History of Maryland Colony, 1634–1776*. Chicago: Raintree, 2005.

Zagarri, Rosemarie. "Slavery in Colonial British North America." Teaching History.org. http://teachinghistory.org/history-content/ask-a-historian/25577

ON THE INTERNET

"13 Colonies Facts." Soft Schools.com. http://www.softschools.com/facts/13_colonies/

"Colonial Children's Games." Pencader Heritage.org. http://www.pencaderheritage.org/main/teachtool/games.pdf

"Daily Life in the American Colonies – Colonial Homes." 13 Colonies Mr. Donn.org. http://13colonies.mrdonn.org/homes.html

"Life in the Southern Colonies." All Things Liberty.com. https://allthingsliberty.com/2013/01/life-in-the-southern-colonies-part-1-of-3/

"The Thirteen American Colonies." Social Studies for Kids.com. http://www.socialstudiesforkids.com/articles/ushistory/13colonies1.htm

GLOSSARY

amicable (AM-i-ka-bl)–friendly, kind

boycott (BOI-kot)–to join with others to refuse to buy something, usually to show disapproval or to force a change in behavior

cask (KASK)–a wooden barrel

convert (kon-VERT)–to change, as in to change from one religion to another

cooper (KOO-per)–someone who makes or repairs wooden barrels or casks

denomination (dee-nom-ih-NAY-shun)–religious group with similar beliefs

destination (des-ti-NAY-shun)–the end point

dire (DIRE)–extreme, usually pertains to something bad

elaborate (ee-LAB-uh-rut)–made with great care or detail

exiled (EGG-zyld)–forced to leave one's home or country

flogged (FLAHGD)–beaten or whipped with a rod or a stick

goods (gudz)– manufactured products

grievances (GREE-vuhn-suhz)–complaints

influenza (in-flu-EHN-zuh)–a contagious virus that makes people very sick (the "flu")

investor (in-VESS-tuhr)–someone who lays out money for a new business, expecting to earn a profit if the business succeeds

latrine (luh-TREEN)– toilet, usually outdoors

monarch (MAHN-ark)– king, ruler

muff (MUHF)–a soft, thick tubelike covering into which both hands can be inserted to keep them warm in cold weather

putrid (PYU-trid)–rotting

Satan (SAY-tan)–another name for the devil

slaver (SLAY-vuhr)–a person involved with the buying and selling of slaves

sloped (SLOWPT)–slanted

smallpox (SMAWL-pawks)–a virus that makes people very sick and often results in death

stocks (STAHKS)–wooden frames with holes for the hands and feet of a wrongdoer used as a form of public punishment in colonial times

succumb (suh-KUHM)–to give in to pressure

tract (TRAKT)–a large piece of land

trencher (TREN-shuhr)–a wooden plate for food

venison (VEHN-ih-son)–deer meat

PHOTO CREDITS: All design elements from Thinkstock/Sharon Beck. Cover, pp. 1, 4, 36—Library of Congress; p. 9—Courtesy of Paris, France Sewer Museum/Audrey Ades; pp. 10, 13, 15, 17, 18, 20, 28, 34—North Wind Picture Archives/Alamy Stock Photo; p. 25—North Wind Picture Archives; p. 33—Royal Albert Museum, Exeter/Public domain; p. 34—(inset)—Public domain.

INDEX

About the Author

As an adult, Audrey Ades developed a love for history and now wishes she had paid more attention in school. These days, she reads lots of history books and has written several about people who have left their marks on the world in quiet but important ways. She has been published by Chicken Soup for the Soul, Schoolwide, and Bumples Magazine. Audrey lives in Florida with her husband and son, who both know a lot about history, and her Pomeranian, Cookie, who doesn't seem to know much at all.